It's Praying Time!

&

NO MORE IDOLS!
Inspired By: God the Father
Written By: Dr. Kimberly K. Clayton

It's Praying Time! & No More Idols!

Copyright © 2021 by Dr. Kimberly K Clayton

ISBN 978-0-578-96012-8

Self-Published Amazon KDP: Dr. Kimberly K. Clayton

itsprayingtime2020@gmail.com
Scriptures are noted from the following versions:

KJV – King James Version

NKJV – New King James Version

NLT – New Living Translation

AMP – Amplified

AMPC – Amplified Classic

GNT – Good News Translation

MSG – The Message Translation

NLV – New Life Version

TPT – The Passion Translation

All rights reserved. No part of this book may be reproduced, stored in a retrieval system, or transmitted by any means or any form: electronic, mechanical, photocopy, recording, or any other, without permission in writing from the author.

Printed in the United States of America

Dr. Kimberly K. Clayton's Books:

1) It's Praying Time - What You Need to Know About Prayer Intercession

2) It's Praying Time & Soul Winning Time!

3) It's Praying Time & Humility is Required!

Dedication

I like to dedicate this book to my late mother, Mrs. Millicent Jones who taught me that no one was above God the Father. You made sure we understood that God was a jealous God, and that no one could sit in his place or try to take his place.

Also to my daughter, Elise who even at a young age has shown a heart for God. Precious Elise I was really blessed that you were alarmed that a Gospel song said, "no one likes the Lord" when actually it was saying "There's Nobody like the Lord". Your loyalty to God shines at a very early age.

I also dedicate this book to my Grandmothers, Willene, Gracie and my bonus Grandmother (Great Aunt) Mary ☺. I have been extremely blessed to have praying Grandmothers like you, that pray and intercede for me and love me the way that you do!

Acknowledgments

I would like to acknowledge God the Father, God the Son (Jesus Christ) and The Holy Spirit for their unconditional love and patience with me. I am forever grateful for all that God has done for me. Thank you for bringing the right people at the right time into my life. God I see you working in my life and I thank you for never giving up on me.

I am thankful for my earthly Dad, Mr. Jones who would encourage me not to give up and to keep going even when I was hard hit by circumstances in life.

To those of you who are apart of "It's Praying Time", I thank you for your faithfulness to pray with me, and for me and Elise. You too have become a part of our spiritual journey and I honor you for that.

Lastly to every faithful and humble Servant of God dedicated to do the work of the Lord, I see your loyalty to God the Father. Please know your labor of love is not in vain, continue to put God first in spite of what others may think or say about you. I commend and celebrate your fervent commitment to God, keep running for Jesus and don't give up now. May you be encouraged and strengthened for the journey ahead, and know that I applaud you and stand in the gap for you!

Table of Contents

Introduction	Pg. 11
Chapter 1: What are Idols & Idolatry?	Pg. 14
Chapter 2: Who Should Avoid Idol Worship?	Pg. 25
Chapter 3: Why are Idols & Idolatry a Sin?	Pg. 34
Chapter 4: How Do We Avoid Idolatry?	Pg. 58
Chapter 5: When Does Idolatry Occur?	Pg. 67
Chapter 6: Where Does Idolatry Happen?	Pg. 75
Chapter 7: Summary & Salvation Prayer	Pg. 93
Author's Biography	Pg. 101

Introduction

Have you noticed how much idolatry and idol worship takes place in the world today? There is no shortage of worshipping people, places, things, guns, power, and of course money.

It is becoming more common place for people to even find substitutes to actually serving, loving and obeying the true and living God. Maybe in the times we live in, it does not seem like a sin or serious offense to worship celebrities, sports, concerts, positions, money, material positions, etc. Yet, the real reality is it is a very serious offense before God. In fact it's one of the Ten Commandments, and is listed as the first of the Ten Commandments.

Although society has changed drastically over the years, God has not. God's words, ways and character remain unchanged, even though humanity is losing its way and getting further from him. Whenever people, try to make a God out of a person isn't it interesting how much chaos comes from that? Believe me that is no coincidence, no one individual will stand in the place of God without serious consequences.

Sometimes society can even use the word idol and hero interchangeably, but even that is an error that should not be made. At one point in time it would be very common to hear people ask someone, "Who is your hero?" but now you hear, "Who is your idol?" For those who don't know any better that's one thing, but people who are Believers in Christ Jesus should know that is not okay. What we don't stand up for now, will be what we regret later.

A question I will ask you throughout this book is, **"Who or what can stand in the place of the true and living God?"**

We want to make the most of every opportunity to win souls for Jesus Christ. The truth is eternity is closer for some than others. We are not just living for this life, but we are surely living for the life to come. Let me encourage you do not delay in saying this Salvation Prayer. Please repeat this prayer from a sincere heart.

Dear Lord Jesus, I know that I am a sinner, and I ask you for your forgiveness. I believe you died for my sins and rose from the dead. I turn from my sins, and invite You to come into my heart and life. I ask for the Holy Spirit to dwell in me, to guide me, and to teach me all things. I choose to trust and follow You as the Son of God and LORD and Savior in Jesus name Amen and Amen.

If you repeated that prayer with a true sincerity you JUST GOT SAVED!!! We encourage you to read your Bible on a daily basis. You can download the Bible App at https://www.youversion.com/the-bible-app/. It will bless you greatly to be able to take the Bible with you everywhere you go. It even allows you to download offline versions of the Bible so you can still read the Bible without Internet access. This Bible App even reads the Bible to you, has devotionals, Bible study plans, prayers and more. Please get a paper Parallel Study Bible that has King James Version(KJV) and New Living Translation(NLT), or another version of your choice that helps you to understand the scriptures.

We are praying with you because getting saved is just the first step. Reading the Bible every day is the second step and the third step is to pray and ask God the Father to lead you to a church home where you will be planted, rooted and established in the Word of God. A good church home that teaches and preaches the Bible without watering it down. Many churches are still working for the Lord even if the doors of the church building are not physically open yet.

Lastly if you repeated the Salvation Prayer and got saved please email us at itsprayingtime2020@gmail.com, we would like to pray for you and encourage you along your spiritual journey. You can also email us your prayer requests and we would be glad to stand in the gap for you.

Chapter 1
What Are Idols & Idolatry?

What are idols? What is idolatry? Dictionary.com defines idol as an image or representation of a god used as an object of worship or a person or thing that is greatly admired, loved or revered. Dictionary.com also lists the following synonyms for idol: icon, god, image, likeness, fetish, totem, statue, figure, figurine, doll, carving, graven image, false god, effigy, golden calf, hero, heroine, star, superstar, icon, celebrity, celebutante, favorite, darling, beloved, pet, pinup, and heart throb. Dictionary.com defines idolatry as the worship of idols or extreme admiration, love, or reverence for something or someone. Dictionary.com lists the following synonyms for idolatry: fetishism, iconolatry, paganism, heathenism, heresy, sacrilege, ungodliness, idolization, idolizing, fetishization, worship, worshipping, adulation, adoration, adoring, reverence, glorification, lionizing, lionization, love, admiration, loving, admiring, and hero-worshipping. Dictionary.com did an excellent job of defining idol and idolatry, along with the numerous synonyms. Even I was amazed to see that hero and heroine were actual synonyms for the word idol.

Father God of all creation and that includes humanity, created us with purposes in mind. One of the purposes is to worship God Almighty. I like the expression that says, "If the purpose of something is not known it will be abused, misused, and neglected." I'll go a step further and say it will even be perverted by the enemy. Just think about the times when people did not bother to read the instruction manual to a device, and they began to use it in ways it was not intended to be used. What happened? It wasn't long before the device began to show signs it was malfunctioning, breaking down and ultimately stop working altogether.

There's a reason that King Solomon the wisest of the Kings and in all of the land was warned by God not to marry foreign wives. God knew it would be just a matter of time before King Solomon's true worship of him (God the Father) would be turned to foreign gods and paganism.

So, in the times that we live in, it makes sense that we should read and study the instruction manual that Father God has left us. When we get to the place and fully embrace that the Bible is not just great stories, but these are events that have actually taken place. We must read and study so we can learn and properly apply the scriptures to our individual lives. If we don't study what the Bible says about idols and idolatry then we are setting ourselves up for failure. The enemy does not play fair, it does not matter that you don't know something, the enemy will use it against you. No one person can know all that there is to know about everything in the Bible, however that is not an excuse to avoid learning what you can.

We were designed to worship God the Father and only God the Father. What you worship is truly what you love. Remember it's not enough to say verbally that you love God the Father, your actions must follow suit also. Dictionary.com defines worship as the feeling or expression of reverence and adoration for a deity or show reverence and adoration for a (a deity), honor with religious rites. Here are some of the synonyms that Dictionary.com listed reverence, adoration, revere, honor, adore and praise. When we truly worship God the Father then we are fulfilling one of our purposes.

Remember God will not come second place, his word informs us that we have to choose whom we will worship, serve, love; and my prayer is that we will always choose wisely and worship God the Father first and him only. Matthew 6:24 KJV *No man can serve two masters: for either he will hate the one, and love the other; or else he will hold to the one, and despise the other. Ye cannot serve God and mammon.* Many years ago there was a popular radio show and then TV show titled Father Knows Best, where the dad really was the patriarch of the family. I like to say it this way "Father God Knows Best", so since he does it is in my best interest to do what he says; obey him without resisting him.

God deserves our true love, adoration, praise, honor and respect above everyone and everything else. Since we are created to worship God only we have to be careful to avoid the temptation to worship anyone or anything else. Sometimes we don't fully understand the consequences of not obeying God; disobedience opens the door to be used by the enemy. When someone refuses to obey God and won't worship him, it won't be long before they are worshipping their spouse, children, supervisor, celebrities, money, or someone or something else.

Whoever or whatever we put in the place of God is an idol, whoever or whatever we worship instead of God is idolatry. Exodus 20:3-6 NKJV *"You shall have no other gods before Me. "You shall not make for yourself a carved image—any likeness of anything that is in heaven above, or that is in the earth beneath, or that is in the water under the earth; you shall not bow down to them nor serve them. For I, the LORD your God, am a jealous God, visiting the iniquity of the fathers upon the children to the third and fourth generations of those who hate Me, but showing mercy to thousands, to those who love*

Me and keep My commandments. As we read this scripture we see that God is real clear about not worshipping or serving other gods.

Have you noticed how excited fans get about basketball games and football games. There is no shortage of yelling, shouting, screaming, jumping up and down, waiving large signs at these games. As believers we have to be the light and lead the way, if one does all of that at a basketball or football game then we have to do even more for God. Let this serve as a reminder and encouragement that the world should not dictate to us about our praise and worship for God.

I noticed that some people know just about everything about celebrities, yet when it comes to the things of God their overall knowledge is very limited. If one is a Believer of Christ Jesus that has to change. We can like and admire people, but we must guard our hearts, thoughts, decisions, and actions on how much attention, adoration, and love we lavish on them. If our conversation is consistently about money, celebrities, material possessions, sports, athletes then it's time for a major change. The world knows how to glorify its own, Believers must know how to glorify God the Father that much more, especially in these last and evil days.

Now let's look at what more of the scriptures say about idols and idolatry. Isaiah 44:9-20 NLT *How foolish are those who manufacture idols. These prized objects are really worthless.*

The people who worship idols don't know this, so they are all put to shame. Who but a fool would make his own god—an idol that cannot help him one bit? All who worship idols will be disgraced along with all these craftsmen—mere humans—who claim they can make a god. They may all stand together, but they will stand in terror and shame. The blacksmith stands at his forge to make a sharp tool, pounding and shaping it with all his might. His work makes him hungry and weak. It makes him thirsty and faint. Then the wood-carver measures a block of wood and draws a pattern on it. He works with chisel and plane and carves it into a human figure. He gives it human beauty and puts it in a little shrine. He cuts down cedars; he selects the cypress and the oak; he plants the pine in the forest to be nourished by the rain. Then he uses part of the wood to make a fire. With it he warms himself and bakes his bread. Then—yes, it's true—he takes the rest of it and makes himself a god to worship! He makes an idol and bows down in front of it! He burns part of the tree to roast his meat and to keep himself warm. He says, "Ah, that fire feels good." Then he takes what's left and makes his god: a carved idol! He falls down in front of it, worshiping and praying to it. "Rescue me!" he says. "You are my god!" Such stupidity and ignorance! Their eyes are closed, and they cannot see. Their minds are shut, and they cannot think. The person who made the idol never stops to reflect, "Why, it's just a block of wood! I burned half of it for heat and used it to bake my bread and roast my meat. How can the rest of it be a god? Should I bow down to worship a piece of wood?" The poor, deluded fool feeds on ashes. He trusts something that can't help him at all. Yet he cannot bring himself to ask, "Is this idol that I'm holding in my hand a lie?"

Jeremiah 1:16 NLT *I will pronounce judgment on my people for all their evil—for deserting me and burning incense to other gods. Yes, they worship idols made with their own hands!*

Daniel 5:23 NLT *For you have proudly defied the Lord of heaven and have had these cups from his Temple brought before you. You and your nobles and your wives and concubines have been drinking wine from them while praising gods of silver, gold, bronze, iron, wood, and stone—gods that neither see nor hear nor know anything at all. But you have not honored the God who gives you the breath of life and controls your destiny!*

Psalm 115:4-8 KJV *Their idols are silver and gold, the work of men's hands. They have mouths, but they speak not: eyes have they, but they see not: They have ears, but they hear not: noses have they, but they smell not: They have hands, but they handle not: feet have they, but they walk not: neither speak they through their throat. They that make them are like unto them; so is every one that trusteth in them.*

The scriptures consistently show us that God says idols are made by man's hands and are worshipped in the place of God; or worshipping gods that are not real, animals, and other creations of God. Even today people are making statues and praising, worshipping and bowing down to them. God's word also makes it clear that honor, praise and adoration giving to idols is indeed idolatry. We have to remember that God has reserved certain things just for him. God has his commandments and warnings about idols and idolatry for a reason. In Chapter 3 Why are Idols & Idolatry A Sin? explains why God has given such stern warnings against idols and idolatry.

It's time to think with the end in mind. **Who or what can stand in the place of the true and living God?** Now that there is a better understanding of idols and idolatry do we really want to worship idols instead of God? We understand that even if we are not making actual idols with our hands that anyone or anything that gets more of our love, time and attention than God the Father is indeed an idol. Our true devotion is reserved for Father God and no one else. We have to have a determined mind that our spouse, children, relatives, pets, jobs, careers, businesses, money, titles, athletes, celebrities, paganism, etc. will not be idols or a source of idolatry in our lives.

In these last and evil days we have to be even more determined to give God the glory, honor and praise that is truly due his name. Remember God the Father won't take third, fourth, fifth place and definitely won't take second place in our lives. The consequences of idols and idolatry are serious and we no longer want to take God's loving grace and mercy for granted. Time is winding down and it is important that we know what idols and idolatry is, so we can avoid it. Say the following prayer with a sincere heart.

Heavenly Father I thank you for your loving kindness towards me. I ask humbly Lord God that you would show me what are the idols and sources of idolatry in my life? Would you please give me the strength to release any and all idols and idolatry in my life? Father God if it is still not clear to me what idols and idolatry are, please open my understanding in a way that only you can, so I won't be deceived by the enemy. Father God thank you in advance for increasing my knowledge on the commandments against idols and idolatry. Would you bless me with a SUPERNATURAL VIGILANCE to avoid idols and idolatry? Father God I ask that you would increase my devotion and adoration for you so there is no room for idols or idolatry. Lord God I am seeking to please you and to put you first in every area

of my life, so I thank you in advance for the greater works that you have called me to. I desire to run my race without idols, without idolatry and without any other traps of the enemy. I also ask would you increase my strength to stand stronger for you in these last and evil days? That I would be SUPERNATURALLY BOLD & COURAGEOUS for you Father God. ABBA Father I want to be well pleasing to you and show you the love, praise and worship that you truly deserve in Jesus Mighty Name Amen and Amen.

Chapter 1 Summary

What Are Idols & Idolatry?

- Idols are any person, place or thing that we worship in the place of God.

- Idolatry is the act of giving our love, devotion, adoration, praise and worship to anyone or anything that is not God the Father.

- God's words (scriptures) lets us know that idols are manmade and cannot save us.

- If we refuse to worship God the Father, we will undoubtedly worship an idol.

- Our true worship is reserved for God the Father.

- Study the Bible, the scriptures on idols and idolatry so you can fight back against the enemy.

Chapter 2
Who Should Avoid Idol Worship?

God's children, Believers of Christ Jesus should avoid idol worship. If ever there were a time to be a better example to this lost and dying world, now is that time. People are looking for the true and living God, and since he can't be seen with natural eyes it is of utmost importance that unbelievers see the true and living God in every Christian believer. God's Kingdom call on our lives is so much greater than we could have ever imagined. We have to seek God for a SUPERNATURAL DETERMINATION to carry out our Kingdom purposes and callings before we leave this earth. The days of just living for ourselves and our families, can no longer be. Too many people are leaving here without accepting and knowing that Jesus Christ is the Son of God. Jesus Christ died so they too could have eternal salvation. Selfishness should no longer dominant a Christian believer's life at this point.

Also, the five-fold ministry must be an excellent example in this area. As much is given much is required, therefore if you are an Apostle, Prophet, Prophetess, Evangelist, Pastor or Teacher it is critical that you have no idols or idol worship in your life. When you are God's leader there is room for you to lead the followers astray. That can no longer happen in this dispensation of time. God is counting on his elect to be a shining example of living an idol free life.

The scripture warns us all that we do not want to be a stumbling block, and those who are in the five-fold ministry are HELD TO A HIGHER GOD STANDARD. Therefore, if you are in the five-fold ministry I highly encourage you to do the exercise in Chapter 6 to make sure there are no obvious or hidden idols in your life, especially in these last and evil days. Five-fold ministry let's glorify, exemplify and magnify Father God with our whole hearts, minds and souls. If anyone knows that they have to live this Goldy lifestyle it is indeed the five-fold ministry leaders of God. Be encouraged five-fold ministry God is counting on you to live a life without idols or idol worship.

If only, more would heed the call and tear down the idols or symbolic idols that have dominated their lives for far too long now. Oh what a powerful praise report and testimony one would have to declare that he or she no longer allows idols or idol worship to dominate their lives anymore. To be able to exclaim to the world that one really thought they were doing all that they could for God, but in actuality when they took time to examine their bank statements, receipts, daily calendar/planner it dawned on them, that God the Father was not first place in their lives.

Now, they thank God that they have a SUPERNATURAL DETERMINATION AND MOTIVATION to remove every idol and every form of idol worship from their lives and the lives of their families. They understand what is at stake and they have a SUPERNATURAL SENSE OF URGENCY to do all they can to worship God the Father with their whole heart, mind and soul. *Matthew 22:37-38 KJV Jesus said unto him, Thou shalt love the Lord thy God with all thy heart, and with all thy soul, and with all thy mind. This is the first and great commandment.* God's word is very clear right here, the first and great commandment we are to follow is to love God with our hearts, souls and minds. Remember the first of the Ten Commandments was "**Thou shalt have no other** gods before me. Exodus 20:3 KJV, but Exodus 20:3 NLT makes it clearer, *"You must not have any other god but me."* Who knows what's best for us? God the Father does, there is no getting around God's wisdom and commandments for our lives.

We have to understand that the Bible, God's Holy Breathed Inspired Word is not just a Biblical Historical Artifact, his Holy Word is for now and every day of our lives. Every Christian Believer needs a fuller and deeper understanding of God's word when it says, "You must not have any other god but me." God the Father is being very direct and to the point with us. When God says something you can bank on it, so we have to understand that God and his Holy Word are both indeed SUPERNATURALLY SOVEREIGN! That means God the Father and his Holy Word have the final say on any and all matters. When we resist this truthful fact and statement, life can be so much harder for us than it really has to be. God the Father is control and in charge, and when he tells us something he knows what happens if there are no instructions, no rules, no guidance; there would be total and ultimate chaos and pandemonium in our lives.

See the enemy may be able to tempt you into idol worship, yet he doesn't tell you the full consequence of your decisions and sins. This is why it is important to know more than enough scripture so the enemy cannot come and deceive you with part of a scripture or scripture completely taken out of context. The saying, "What you don't know, can't hurt you.", is not true when it comes to God's Holy Word, as believers we still need to know the Bible for ourselves. The times that we live in we can't keep saying that we did not know what God requires of us when we have access to printed Bibles, digital Bibles and Internet Bibles too. This is the time to go higher in Jesus Christ, not lower; this is the time to cling and hold on to God the Father, not fall away. So be encouraged and do all that you can as a believer to study the scriptures on idols and idolatry (idol worship). The enemy knows that if you don't know God's Holy Word he can and will use it completely against you.

Another viewpoint is this, when the enemy tricks you into idolatry then he can distract you from your true love and devotion to God the Father. The enemy does not mind you saying verbally that you love God, that you love Jesus as long as he can get your actions to be contrary to your words then he knows that he won. One of the enemies greatest deception is to trick a believer into thinking that his or her verbal words are enough for God, but that's not true. If we really love God we will obey him and do what his Holy Word says. Obedience is faith.

How can we say we trust and believe in God Almighty, but outright refuse to do what he says on a consistent basis? When God tell us to love and worship him only, we have to obey him. God knows that if our devotion is not totally to him, that we leave the door open for the enemy to come in and attack us. He knows that the enemy does not play fair and that he can keep our focus on the wrong thing like idolatry, he can get us to commit a lot of other sins. It wouldn't be long before we had completely fallen away and yet think we are totally devoted to God.

The same is true about attending church, the enemy does not mind you going to church as long as he knows that the true church is not in you (or your heart, mind and soul). Saints of old would often let us know it's not enough just to go to church, you have to become the church. It takes consistent reading, meditating, praying and living God's Holy Word to mature and to fulfill God's word concerning our individual lives. Yes, faith is what you believe God for and hasn't materialized yet; it also an action where we obey God through our actions, works and waiting seasons in life.

God is calling us (the Body of Christ) higher, and it requires us to leave behind every idol and all forms of idol worship. Again I ask you, **Who or what will stand in the place of the true and living God in your life?** Can you be counted on as a Believer to give up idolatry in your life at every level? Self-reflection should take place on a daily basis, to help us to be more aware of where we are doing well and where we need improvement.

When the Holy Spirit convicts us, especially of idol worship it doesn't feel good. However, it is a very necessary part of our spiritual growth in a personal relationship with Jesus Christ and Father God. When we are convicted that's the time to come clean with God and ask him to help us to get rid of all idols and idolatry in our lives. God the Father is there for us, but we must be willing to come to him when we sin against him by not obeying his commandments. Are you willing to partner with Father God, Jesus Christ and the Holy Spirit to be delivered totally from all idols and idol worship? In Chapter 6 there is an exercise that will help you to see where your idols are. Also, here is a prayer to help you start on this journey renouncing of all idols and idol worship.

Heavenly Father thank you for this journey of renouncing and denouncing all idols that are in my life. Please reveal to me any and all idols and idolatry that is currently taking place in my life. I desire to please you Lord God with my whole heart, mind and soul and ask that you would give me the strength to embrace, love and worship you only Father God. Lord, would you increase my discernment so that the enemy cannot deceive me into thinking that I am devoted to you, when I am not? Would you help me Lord God not to override the Holy Spirit when he convicts me? As time is winding down could you please help me to have a SUPERNATURAL SENSE OF URGENCY to let go of all idols and idol worship immediately? Would you help me to stand boldly for you at all times in spite of what others may think or say? Lord I need your assistance with daily self-reflection to help keep me on track with my spiritual growth and my personal relationship with you. Father God would you help me to thirst for the righteousness of your Holy Word on a daily basis? I

have no doubt that you will fill me with righteousness because your word says those who thirst for righteousness will be filled. As I learn the importance of your commandments help me to honor the First Commandment and the Greatest Commandment of all is to have no other God but you and to love you, Father God with my whole heart, mind and soul. I understand when I read your Holy Word (the Bible) that it is speaking to me and I must strive to obey your word on a daily basis. Help me Lord to understand that my obedience is my faith, that I demonstrate my faith through obedience to you, Father God and your commandments. Help me to answer the call to go HIGHER IN CHRIST JESUS, that I am not ashamed to own the name of Jesus Christ before others. Father God I desire to be the Kingdom Leader you are calling me to be, and understand that my life is not my own and I have a SUPERNATURAL CALL, DUTY AND OBLIGATION TO SERVE YOU WHOLEHEARTEDLY BEFORE YOU AND PEOPLE ON A CONSISTENT BASIS IN JESUS MIGHTY NAME AMEN AND AMEN.

Chapter 2 – Summary

Who Should Avoid Idol Worship?

- **EVERYONE**

- **Especially the five-fold ministry: Apostles, Prophets, Evangelists, Pastors, Teachers**

- **The world is watching, we must be the example that God has always called for.**

- **Our faith is demonstrated through obedience.**

- **Our actions determine if we are really devoted to God, not what we say verbally.**

- **Asking God for help in this area, is indeed necessary.**

- **When the Holy Spirit convicts us don't override him, go straight to God in prayer.**

Chapter 3
Why are Idols & Idol Worship A Sin?

So, why are idols and idol worship a sin? Simply put because Father God says so and knows what is best for us. Let's look at a brief review of the children of Israel and God the Father. When one studies the Old Testament it is evident to see that the children of Israel had serious faithfulness and obedience issues. If you haven't reviewed the book of Judges in a while, now is a good time to go back and review it. God's faithfulness is demonstrated throughout the Bible in both the Old Testament and New Testament. Yet in Judges it is in full display that as long as the children of Israel would obey God they lived blessed and prosperous lives. Unfortunately when the children of Israel disobeyed God their lives were full of punishment through being oppressed and full of hardship.

Amazingly as the children of Israel cried out to God about the oppression and even the harsh cruelties of slavery, God was always faithful to raise up a Judge a true deliverer for them. God's wrath toward the children of Israel never lasted forever and that's a true testament to God's ability to chastise them, but yet forgive and restore them as well. Yet, overall when the children of Israel would cry out seldom would they say to God, please help us to obey or even promise to obey that they would be faithful to him. God demonstrates an unconditional love for the children of Israel that he delivers them even when he knows that their obedience and faithfulness to him is temporary and won't last long.

*Judges 2:11-23 NLT The Israelites did evil in the L*ORD*'s sight and served the images of Baal. They abandoned the L*ORD*, the God of their ancestors, who had brought them out of Egypt. They went after other gods, worshiping the gods of the people around them. And they angered the L*ORD*. They abandoned the L*ORD *to serve Baal and the images of Ashtoreth. This made the L*ORD *burn with anger against Israel, so he handed them over to raiders who stole their possessions. He turned them over to their enemies all around, and they were no longer able to resist them. Every time Israel went out to battle, the L*ORD *fought against them, causing them to be defeated, just as he had warned. And the people were in great distress. Then the L*ORD *raised up judges to rescue the Israelites from their attackers. Yet Israel did not listen to the judges but prostituted themselves by worshiping other gods. How quickly they turned away from the path of their ancestors, who had walked in obedience to the L*ORD*'s commands. Whenever the L*ORD *raised up a judge over Israel, he was with that* *judge and rescued the people from their enemies throughout the judge's lifetime. For the LORD took pity on his people, who were burdened by oppression and suffering. But when the judge died, the people returned to their corrupt ways, behaving worse than those who had lived before them. They went after other gods, serving and worshiping them. And they refused to give up their evil practices and stubborn ways. So the LORD burned with anger against Israel. He said, "Because these people have violated my covenant, which I made with their ancestors, and have ignored my commands, I will no longer drive out the nations that Joshua left unconquered when he died. I did this to test Israel—to see whether or not they would follow the ways of the LORD as their ancestors did." That is why the LORD left those nations in place. He did not quickly drive them out or allow Joshua to conquer them all.*

As you have been on this journey with me I hope that you can see I like to study the Biblical patriarchs and matriarchs, and what they were known for. So we will turn our attention to King Solomon, who was known for being the wisest and that there would be no one wiser than him. Let's look at what the scriptures say about Solomon's wisdom:

1 Kings 3:5-28 AMP **In Gibeon the LORD appeared to Solomon in a dream at night; and God said, "Ask [Me] what I shall give you."** Then Solomon said, "You have

shown Your servant David my father great lovingkindness, because he walked before You in faithfulness and righteousness and with uprightness of heart toward You; and You have kept for him this great lovingkindness, in that You have given him a son to sit on his throne, as it is today. So now, O LORD my God, You have made Your servant king in place of David my father; and as for me, I am but a little boy [in wisdom and experience]; I do not know how to go out or come in [that is, how to conduct business as a king]. Your servant is among Your people whom You have chosen, a great people who are too many to be numbered or counted. **So give Your servant an understanding mind and a hearing heart [with which] to judge Your people, so that I may discern between good and evil. For who is able to judge and rule this great people of Yours?"** *Now it pleased the Lord that Solomon had asked this thing.* **God said to him, "Because you have asked this and have not asked for yourself a long life nor for wealth, nor for the lives of your enemies, but have asked for yourself understanding to recognize justice, behold, I have done as you asked. I have given you a wise and discerning heart (mind), so that no one before you was your equal, nor shall anyone equal to you arise after you.** *I have also given you what you have not asked, both wealth and honor, so that there will not be anyone equal to you among the kings, for all your days.* **If you walk in My ways, keeping My statutes and My commandments, as your father David did, then I will lengthen your days."**

Then Solomon awoke, and he realized that it was a dream. He came [back] to Jerusalem and stood before the ark of the covenant of the L ORD*; he offered burnt offerings and peace offerings, and he prepared a feast for all his servants Then two women who were prostitutes came to the king and stood before him. And the one woman said, "O my lord, this woman and I live in the same house; and I gave birth to a child while she was in the house. And on the third day after I gave birth, this woman also gave birth. And we were [alone] together; no one else was with us in the house, just we two. Now this woman's son died during the night, because she lay on him [and smothered him]. So she got up in the middle of the night and took my son from [his place] beside me while your maidservant was asleep, and laid him on her bosom, and laid her dead son on my bosom. When I got up in the morning to nurse my son, behold, he was dead. But when I examined him carefully in the morning, behold, it was not my son, the one whom I had borne." Then the other woman said, "No! For my son is the one who is living, and your son is the dead one." But the first woman said, "No! For your son is the dead one, and my son is the living one." [This is how] they were speaking before the king. Then the king said, "This woman says, 'This is my son, the one who is alive, and your son is the dead one'; and the other woman says, 'No! For your son is the dead one, and my son is the one who is alive.'"* **Then the king said, "Bring me a sword." So they brought a sword before the king. Then the king**

said, "Cut the living child in two, and give half to the one [woman] and half to the other." Then the woman whose child was the living one spoke to the king, for she was deeply moved over her son, "O my lord, give her the living child, and by no means kill him." But the other said, "He shall be neither mine nor yours; cut him!" **Then the king said, "Give the first woman [who is pleading for his life] the living child, and by no means kill him. She is his mother." When all [the people of] Israel heard about the judgment which the king had made, they [were in awe and reverently] feared the king, for they saw that the wisdom of God was within him to administer justice.**

1 Kings 4:29-34 AMP *Now God gave Solomon [exceptional] wisdom and very great discernment and breadth of mind, like the sand of the seashore. Solomon's wisdom surpassed the wisdom of all the sons of the east and all the wisdom of Egypt. For he was wiser than all [other] men, [wiser] than Ethan the Ezrahite, and Heman, Calcol, and Darda, the sons of Mahol. His fame was known in all the surrounding nations. He also spoke 3,000 proverbs, and his songs were 1,005. He spoke of trees, from the cedar which is in Lebanon to the hyssop [vine] that grows on the wall; he spoke also of animals, of birds, of creeping things, and fish. People came from all the peoples (nations) to hear the wisdom of Solomon, and from all the kings of the earth who had heard of his wisdom.*

1 Kings 5:7 AMP *When Hiram heard the words of Solomon, he rejoiced greatly and said, "Blessed be the LORD this day, who has given David a wise son [to be king] over this great people."*

1 Kings 10:1-10 AMP *Now when the queen of Sheba heard of the fame of Solomon concerning the name of the LORD, she came to test him with riddles. So she came to Jerusalem with a very large caravan (entourage), with camels carrying spices, a great quantity of gold, and precious stones. When she came to Solomon, she spoke with him about everything that was on her mind [to discover the extent of his wisdom]. Solomon answered all her questions; there was nothing hidden from the king which he did not explain to her. When the queen of Sheba had seen all the wisdom of Solomon, and the house (palace) which he had built, the food on his table, the seating of his servants (court officials), the attendance of his waiters and their attire, his cupbearers, his stairway by which he went up to the house (temple) of the LORD, she was breathless and awed [by the wonder of it all]. Then she told the king, "The report which I heard in my own land about your words and wisdom is true! I did not believe the report until I came and saw it with my own eyes. Behold, the half of it was not told to me. You exceed in wisdom and prosperity the report which I heard. How blessed (fortunate, happy) are your men! How blessed are these your servants who stand continually before you, hearing your wisdom!*

Blessed be the LORD your God who delighted in you to set you on the throne of Israel! Because the LORD loved Israel forever, He made you king to execute justice and righteousness." She gave the king a hundred and twenty talents of gold and a very great quantity of spices and precious stones. Never again did such an abundance of spices come in [to Israel] as that which the queen of Sheba gave King Solomon.

God also gave King Solomon specific instructions on how he should obey him and warnings on not serving other Gods. 1 Kings 6:12 KJV *Concerning this house which thou art in building, if thou wilt walk in my statutes, and execute my judgments, and keep all my commandments to walk in them; then will I perform my word with thee, which I spake unto David thy father:*

1 Kings 3:14 KJV *And if thou wilt walk in my ways, to keep my statutes and my commandments, as thy father David did walk, then I will lengthen thy days.*

1 Kings 9:1-9 AMP *Now it happened when Solomon had finished building the house (temple) of the LORD and the king's house (palace), and all else which he was pleased to do, that the LORD appeared to Solomon a second time, just as He had appeared to him at Gibeon. The LORD told him, "I have heard your prayer and supplication which you have made before Me; I have consecrated this house which you have built by putting My Name and My*

Presence there forever. My eyes and My heart shall be there perpetually. As for you, if you walk (live your life) before Me, as David your father walked, in integrity of heart and in uprightness, acting in accordance with everything that I have commanded you, and will keep My statutes and My precepts, then I will establish the throne of your kingdom over Israel forever, just as I promised your father David, saying, 'You shall not be without a man (descendant) on the throne of Israel.'
*"But if you or your sons turn away from following Me, and do not keep My commandments and My statutes which I have set before you, but go and serve other gods and worship them, then I will cut off Israel from the land which I have given them, and I will cast out of My sight the house which I have consecrated for My Name and Presence. Then Israel will become a proverb (a saying) and a byword (object of ridicule) among all the peoples. This house (temple) will become a heap of ruins; everyone who passes by will be appalled and sneer and say, 'Why has the L*ORD *done such a thing to this land and to this house?' And they [who know] will say, 'Because they abandoned the L*ORD *their God, who brought their fathers out of the land of Egypt, and they have chosen other gods and have worshiped and served them; that is the reason the L*ORD *has brought on them all this adversity.'"*

Even King David reminded King Solomon of what God required of him so the promises of God would be

fulfilled. 1 Kings 2:1-4 AMP *When David's time to die approached, he gave instructions to Solomon his son, saying, "I am going the way of all the earth [as dust to dust]. Be strong and prove yourself a man. Keep the charge of the LORD your God, [that is, fulfill your obligation to] walk in His ways, keep His statutes, His commandments, His precepts, and His testimonies, as it is written in the Law of Moses, so that you may succeed in everything that you do and wherever you turn, so that the LORD may fulfill His promise concerning me, saying, 'If your sons are careful regarding their way [of life], to walk before Me in truth with all their heart and mind and with all their soul, you shall not fail to have a man (descendant) on the throne of Israel.'*

The children of Israel were warned about marrying foreigners because God knew they would eventually turn their hearts from serving him, to serving idol and pagan gods.

1 Kings 11:1-12 NLT *Now King Solomon loved many foreign women. Besides Pharaoh's daughter, he married women from Moab, Ammon, Edom, Sidon, and from among the Hittites. The LORD had clearly instructed the people of Israel, "You must not marry them, because they will turn your hearts to their gods." Yet Solomon insisted on loving them anyway. He had 700 wives of royal birth and 300 concubines. And in fact, they did turn*

his heart away from the Lord. In Solomon's old age, they turned his heart to worship other gods instead of being completely faithful to the Lord his God, as his father, David, had been. Solomon worshiped Ashtoreth, the goddess of the Sidonians, and Molech, the detestable god of the Ammonites. In this way, Solomon did what was evil in the Lord's sight; he refused to follow the Lord completely, as his father, David, had done. On the Mount of Olives, east of Jerusalem, he even built a pagan shrine for Chemosh, the detestable god of Moab, and another for Molech, the detestable god of the Ammonites. Solomon built such shrines for all his foreign wives to use for burning incense and sacrificing to their gods. The Lord was very angry with Solomon, for his heart had turned away from the Lord, the God of Israel, who had appeared to him twice. He had warned Solomon specifically about worshiping other gods, but Solomon did not listen to the Lord's command. So now the Lord said to him, "Since you have not kept my covenant and have disobeyed my decrees, I will surely tear the kingdom away from you and give it to one of your servants. But for the sake of your father, David, I will not do this while you are still alive. I will take the kingdom away from your son. And even so, I will not take away the entire kingdom; I will let him be king of one tribe, for the sake of my servant David and for the sake of Jerusalem, my chosen city."

As we read this scripture we can see that King Solomon had every intention of following God and his commands, however he had a weakness for foreign women. The scriptures show that even with King Solomon's great wisdom, it did not keep him from making the right choice and avoiding the foreign women. Unfortunately King Solomon was punished, through his son who would only rule part of the kingdom, and not the whole kingdom. God even allowed the peace that King Solomon once enjoyed to come to an end. King Solomon's enemies were allowed to rise up against him.

1 Kings 11:14 NLT *Then the Lord raised up Hadad the Edomite, a member of Edom's royal family, to be Solomon's adversary.*

1 Kings 11:26-40 NLT *Another rebel leader was Jeroboam son of Nebat, one of Solomon's own officials. He came from the town of Zeredah in Ephraim, and his mother was Zeruah, a widow. This is the story behind his rebellion. Solomon was rebuilding the supporting terraces and repairing the walls of the city of his father, David. Jeroboam was a very capable young man, and when Solomon saw how industrious he was, he put him in charge of the labor force from the tribes of Ephraim and Manasseh, the descendants of Joseph. One day as Jeroboam was leaving Jerusalem, the prophet Ahijah from Shiloh met him along the way. Ahijah was wearing a new cloak. The two of them were alone in a field, and*

*Ahijah took hold of the new cloak he was wearing and tore it into twelve pieces. Then he said to Jeroboam, "Take ten of these pieces, for this is what the L*ORD*, the God of Israel, says: 'I am about to tear the kingdom from the hand of Solomon, and I will give ten of the tribes to you! But I will leave him one tribe for the sake of my servant David and for the sake of Jerusalem, which I have chosen out of all the tribes of Israel. For Solomon has abandoned me and worshiped Ashtoreth, the goddess of the Sidonians; Chemosh, the god of Moab; and Molech, the god of the Ammonites. He has not followed my ways and done what is pleasing in my sight. He has not obeyed my decrees and regulations as David his father did. "'But I will not take the entire kingdom from Solomon at this time. For the sake of my servant David, the one whom I chose and who obeyed my commands and decrees, I will keep Solomon as leader for the rest of his life. But I will take the kingdom away from his son and give ten of the tribes to you. His son will have one tribe so that the descendants of David my servant will continue to reign, shining like a lamp in Jerusalem, the city I have chosen to be the place for my name. And I will place you on the throne of Israel, and you will rule over all that your heart desires. If you listen to what I tell you and follow my ways and do whatever I consider to be right, and if you obey my decrees and commands, as my servant David did, then I will always be with you. I will establish an enduring dynasty for you as I did for David, and I will give Israel to you. Because of Solomon's* *sin I will punish the descendants of David—though not forever.'" Solomon tried to kill Jeroboam, but he fled to King Shishak of Egypt and stayed there until Solomon died.*

As we read these scriptures we see that God is very serious about our devotion being to him only. See, the enemy can tempt us into idols and idolatry, but he does not tell us all of the truth or any of the consequences that follow. God not only punishes the person who committed idolatry, but punishes his or her children too. In Old Testament times idolatry often caused the children of Israel to be enslaved and had to endure the cruelty of slavery. God gives us free will but that's not to be abused by us as an excuse to do whatever we want, whenever we want.

The real reality is this, if we really love God like we say we do, then it's not a burden to avoid idols and idol worship. We are glad to give God the glory with our whole heart, mind and soul in spite of what may be going on in our lives. Come what may, we should have determined hearts to live for God and even more vigilant not to allow idols any room in our lives. Remember our actions must line up with what we profess and believe. The question, **Who or what will stand in the place of the true and living God?, cannot be taken lightly. The scripture informs us if you really**

want to provoke the wrath of God, idols and idolatry (idol worship) is the way to do it!

Deuteronomy 4:25-26 KJV *When thou shalt beget children, and children's children, and ye shall have remained long in the land, and shall corrupt yourselves, and make a graven image, or the likeness of anything, and shall do evil in the sight of the LORD thy God, to provoke him to anger: I call heaven and earth to witness against you this day, that ye shall soon utterly perish from off the land whereunto ye go over Jordan to possess it; ye shall not prolong your days upon it, but shall utterly be destroyed.*

Deuteronomy 9:16-19 KJV *And I looked, and, behold, ye had sinned against the LORD your God, and had made you a molten calf: ye had turned aside quickly out of the way which the LORD had commanded you. And I took the two tables, and cast them out of my two hands, and brake them before your eyes. And I fell down before the LORD, as at the first, forty days and forty nights: I did neither eat bread, nor drink water, because of all your sins which ye sinned, in doing wickedly in the sight of the LORD, to provoke him to anger. For I was afraid of the anger and hot displeasure, wherewith the LORD was wroth against you to destroy you. But
the LORD hearkened unto me at that time also.*

1 Kings 22:51-53 KJV *Ahaziah the son of Ahab began to reign over Israel in Samaria the seventeenth year of*

*Jehoshaphat king of Judah, and reigned two years over Israel. And he did evil in the sight of the L*ORD*, and walked in the way of his father, and in the way of his mother, and in the way of Jeroboam the son of Nebat, who made Israel to sin: For he served Baal, and worshipped him, and provoked to anger the L*ORD *God of Israel, according to all that his father had done.*

Psalm 106:28-30 KJV *They joined themselves also unto Baalpeor, and ate the sacrifices of the dead. Thus they provoked him to anger with their inventions: and the plague brake in upon them. Then stood up Phinehas, and executed judgment: and so the plague was stayed.*

Jeremiah 44:3-8 KJV *Because of their wickedness which they have committed to provoke me to anger, in that they went to burn incense, and to serve other gods, whom they knew not, neither they, ye, nor your fathers. Howbeit I sent unto you all my servants the prophets, rising early and sending them, saying, Oh, do not this abominable thing that I hate. But they hearkened not, nor inclined their ear to turn from their wickedness, to burn no incense unto other gods. Wherefore my fury and mine anger was poured forth, and was kindled in the cities of Judah and in the streets of Jerusalem; and they are wasted and desolate, as at this day. Therefore now thus saith the L*ORD*, the God of hosts, the God of Israel; Wherefore commit ye this great evil against your souls, to cut off from you man and woman, child and suckling,* *out of Judah, to leave you none to remain; In that ye provoke me unto wrath with the works of your hands, burning incense unto other gods in the land of Egypt, whither ye be gone to dwell, that ye might cut yourselves off, and that ye might be a curse and a reproach among all the nations of the earth?*

Jeremiah 8:19 NLT *Listen to the weeping of my people; it can be heard all across the land.*
"Has the LORD abandoned Jerusalem?" the people ask. "Is her King no longer there?"
"Oh, why have they provoked my anger with their carved idols and their worthless foreign gods?" says the LORD.

Jeremiah 25:2-11 NLT *Jeremiah the prophet said to all the people in Judah and Jerusalem, "For the past twenty-three years—from the thirteenth year of the reign of Josiah son of Amon, king of Judah, until now—*
the LORD has been giving me his messages. I have faithfully passed them on to you, but you have not listened. "Again and again the LORD has sent you his servants, the prophets, but you have not listened or even paid attention. Each time the message was this: 'Turn from the evil road you are traveling and from the evil things you are doing. Only then will I let you live in this land that the LORD gave to you and your ancestors forever. Do not provoke my anger by worshiping idols you made with your own hands. Then I will not harm you.' "But you would not listen to me," says the LORD.

"You made me furious by worshiping idols you made with your own hands, bringing on yourselves all the disasters you now suffer. And now the LORD of Heaven's Armies says: Because you have not listened to me, I will gather together all the armies of the north under King Nebuchadnezzar of Babylon, whom I have appointed as my deputy. I will bring them all against this land and its people and against the surrounding nations. I will completely destroy you and make you an object of horror and contempt and a ruin forever. I will take away your happy singing and laughter. The joyful voices of bridegrooms and brides will no longer be heard. Your millstones will fall silent, and the lights in your homes will go out. This entire land will become a desolate wasteland. Israel and her neighboring lands will serve the king of Babylon for seventy years.

Psalm 78:55-59 NLT *He drove out the nations before them; he gave them their inheritance by lot. He settled the tribes of Israel into their homes. But they kept testing and rebelling against God Most High. They did not obey his laws. They turned back and were as faithless as their parents. They were as undependable as a crooked bow. They angered God by building shrines to other gods; they made him jealous with their idols. When God heard them, he was very angry, and he completely rejected Israel.*

Judges 3:5-9 KJV *And the children of Israel dwelt among the Canaanites, Hittites, and Amorites, and Perizzites, and Hivites, and Jebusites: And they took their daughters to be their wives, and gave their daughters to their sons, and served their gods. And the children of Israel did evil in the sight of the L*ORD*, and forgat the L*ORD *their God, and served Baalim and the groves. Therefore the anger of the L*ORD *was hot against Israel, and he sold them into the hand of Chushanrishathaim king of Mesopotamia: and the children of Israel served Chushanrishathaim eight years. And when the children of Israel cried unto the L*ORD*, the L*ORD *raised up a deliverer to the children of Israel, who delivered them, even Othniel the son of Kenaz, Caleb's younger brother.*

After reading these scriptures it is easy to see that God's wrath is provoked because of idols and idol worship, worshipping statues, graven images, foreign gods all bring about a very fiery anger from God. And these aren't all of the scriptures on idols and idol worship or the concept of idolatry, there are numerous scriptures and that means that's a very serious topic. Whenever a command, a warning of what happens when the command is violated, and what actually happens is mentioned well over ninety times it is serious and needs our complete attention.

We can even see that the children of Israel would serve faithfully as long as they had a righteous leader (King,

Priest, Judge, Prophet) that served God faithfully and consistently reminded the people of God's faithfulness, goodness and mercy towards them and their ancestors. We can see the value and how important it was for the children of Israel to have righteous leadership that would not lead them astray! This is applicable to our lives today we should be following people who are following Jesus Christ, otherwise there is a very good chance that he or she will lead you astray.

The children of Israel were unfaithful and unfortunately sometimes forgot to teach the next generation the ways of the Lord and his great miracles. When those who followed the Lord eventually died out, there was no longer proper guidance and instructions for the next generation. The children of Israel did not always have righteous leadership and unfortunately certain Kings lead them from the true and living God, to serve idols and foreign gods. God was provoked to anger and it is unfortunate that the children of Israel did not take heed to God's warnings through his words, commandments or through his Prophets either. Even if they would have remembered how God delivered their ancestors from Pharaoh, and what happened when they refused to obey and trust in him. That should have helped them to obey and not turn away from God.

There's a danger in not knowing or remembering the past, that unfortunately it is doomed to be repeated. I thank God that he made sure we had a guide of solid, trustworthy instructions in the Bible. The Bible helps us to see what happened in the past to help us navigate our present and future according to God's principles, instructions and warnings!

Let these scriptures serve as reminders to us that although we may not make idols with our hands, we still don't want any symbolic idols in our lives either. Wherever we spend our time and money will reveal to us our obvious and hidden symbolic idols (See Ch. 6). We don't want idols or idol worship in our lives because there will be very serious consequences if we don't let them go, and turn back to Father God whole heartedly. If we truly love God we will obey him and let's just be frank about it, GOD DESERVES OUR TOTAL LOVE, ADORATION, PRAISE AND GLORY AT ALL TIMES. Our true worship is our everyday lifestyle and we must give God our VERY BEST AND NOTHING LESS.

What job, career, business, even marriage will last if all parties blatantly do whatever they want, whenever they want? NOT SO! So, why do we think we can survive especially in these last and evil days without truly be connected to God Almighty? His Holy Word gives us life and life more abundantly and our worship keeps us connected to his power, love and blessings for our lives. Remember there is a blessing in being obedient. Why should we live beneath our true privileges in God?

Who or what will stand in the place of the true and living God?

Heavenly Father, now that I know that idols and idolatry are a serious sin, with serious consequences please help me to obey the First and Greatest Commandment. I desire to be a Godly example to those who are around me especially children, even those that are not mine too. Father God would you help me to live out the First and Greatest Commandment on a daily basis? Lord God I do not want destruction to come to my life or to the lives of my loved ones. Would you please help me to understand that I have been bought with a price and I am not my own? That Jesus died so we could be saved (inherit eternal life) and be free from all deception of idols and idol worship. Father God I understand that obedience is better than sacrifice; that it's better to obey you and be blessed then to disobey and have to suffer for it. In Jesus Mighty Name Amen and Amen.

Chapter 3 Summary

Why Are Idols & Idol Worship A Sin?

- **Because God the Father says so and knows what's best for us.**

- **Our bad example doesn't just impact us, but our children and future generations.**

- **There are serious consequences for idols and idol worshipping.**

- **It breaks the 1st and Greatest Commandment from God Almighty**
    - You shall not have any other God's before me.
    - You shall love your God with your whole heart, mind and soul.

- **Blatant disobedience will not continually be tolerated by God the Father.**
    - Deuteronomy 8:19-20 NKJV Then it shall be, if you by any means forget the LORD your God, and follow other gods, and serve them and worship them, I testify against you this day that you shall surely perish. As the nations which the LORD destroys before you, so you shall

perish, because you would not be obedient to the voice of the LORD your God.

- **Father God deserves a true devotion and he will not come second place, and definitely not last place!**

  - **Matthew 22:36-38 NLT** *"Teacher, which is the most important commandment in the law of Moses?" Jesus replied, "'You must love the L*ORD *your God with all your heart, all your soul, and all your mind.' This is the first and greatest commandment.*

- **WHO OR WHAT WILL STAND IN THE PLACE OF THE TRUE AND LIVING GOD???**

Chapter 4
How Do We Avoid Idolatry?

How do we avoid idolatry? That's a good question. The answer is simple, keeping God first in every area of our lives. When we keep God first there is no room for idols or idolatry (idol worship) in our lives. When we truly understand the power of the 1st and Greatest Commandment, (Matthew 22:36-38 NLT *"Teacher, which is the most important commandment in the law of Moses?" Jesus replied, "'You must love the LORD your God with all your heart, all your soul, and all your mind.' This is the first and greatest commandment.)* then we will embrace it and allow the power of God to shape and mold us like never before.

Do you have the desire to please God? If not, that's a good place to start in prayer, asking God the Father to give you the desire to please him and to live for him with your whole heart, mind and soul. Pray the 1st and Greatest Commandment every day and watch a DIVINE TURNAROUND come into your life like never before! Prayer is transformative, but it's not always instant…let me encourage you to remain committed to prayer every day. We live in times that we really have to pray without ceasing. Especially when God is revealing and exposing the enemies tactics, those are prayer points and prayer targets that have to be prayed through without fail and without excuses.

Let's look at Psalm 37:4 in a few different translations to gain a fuller understanding of this scripture. Psalm 37:4 KJV *Delight thyself also in the Lord: and he shall give thee the desires of thine heart.*

Psalm 37:4 TPT (The Passion Translation) *Find your delight and true pleasure in Yahweh, and he will give you what you desire the most.*

Psalm 37:4 NLV (New Life Version) *Be happy in the Lord. And He will give you the desires of your heart.*

After reading these scriptures it becomes more clear that when we are truly seeking our happiness and joy in the Lord he will give us the desires of our hearts. Dictionary.com defines delight:

As a verb: to please someone greatly; with the following synonyms: charm, enchant, captivate, entrance, bewitch, thrill, excite.

As a noun: great pleasure; with the following synonyms: pleasure, happiness, joy, joyfulness, glee, gladness, gratification, relish.

Dictionary.com defines desires as a strong feeling of wanting to have something or wishing for something to happen.

So, another way of saying Psalm 37:4 is, When we are captivated with joy, gladness and gratification about the Lord, he will give us those things that we have longed for and/or want to happen. So when you are worshipping the Lord with a joyfulness and thankfulness, when you desire to put God first in every area of your life, God will help this happen. As we grow in our relationship with Christ Jesus we begin to realize that we need more than money, material possession, resources; we need spiritual blessings, insights and strategies to continue to walk by faith and not by sight.

The Body of Christ will have to live in obedience to God the Father. Especially if we are going to live a life that pleases him and brings him the glory on a consistent basis. The consequences of disobedience are intensifying all around us, so let's take heed while we still have the time.

When Jesus told the Samaritan woman at the well how to truly worship God the Father. We will read a few translations of John 4:20-24

KJV *Our fathers worshipped in this mountain; and ye say, that in Jerusalem is the place where men ought to worship. Jesus saith unto her, Woman, believe me, the hour cometh, when ye shall neither in this mountain, nor yet at Jerusalem, worship the Father. Ye worship ye know not what: we know what we worship: for salvation* is of the Jews. But the hour cometh, and now is, when the true worshippers shall worship the Father in spirit and in truth: for the Father seeketh such to worship him. God is a Spirit: and they that worship him must worship him in spirit and in truth.

TPT *So tell me this: Why do our fathers worship God on this nearby mountain, but your people teach that Jerusalem is the place where we must worship. Who is right?" Jesus responded, "Believe me, dear woman, the time has come when you will worship the Father neither on a mountain nor in Jerusalem, but in your heart. Your people don't really know the One they worship, but we Jews worship out of our experience, for it's from the Jews that salvation is available. From now on, worshiping the Father will not be a matter of the right place but with a right heart. For God is a Spirit, and he longs to have sincere worshipers who adore him in the realm of the Spirit and in truth."*

MSG *Well, tell me this: Our ancestors worshiped God at this mountain, but you Jews insist that Jerusalem is the only place for worship, right?" "Believe me, woman, the time is coming when you Samaritans will worship the Father neither here at this mountain nor there in Jerusalem. You worship guessing in the dark; we Jews worship in the clear light of day. God's way of salvation is made available through the Jews. But the time is coming—it has, in fact, come—when what you're called will not matter and where you go to worship will not matter. "It's who you are and the way you live that count before God. Your worship must engage your spirit in the pursuit of truth. That's the kind of people the Father is out looking for: those who are simply and honestly themselves before him in their worship. God is sheer being itself—Spirit. Those who worship him must do it out of their very being, their spirits, their true selves, in adoration."*

How else do you worship God the Father? In spirit and in truth, the scriptures help us to understand that we must have a right heart with God, that we actually live the life that we profess and proclaim before others in public and in private. Are we actually doing what God has commanded us to do? If we are not searching the scriptures on a daily basis, it makes it harder to truly know what God expects of us. We have to put actual effort and work into our Christian faith lifestyle.

What we put into our faith, relationship with Jesus Christ and Father God is what we get out of it. Let me encourage you, do not be afraid or hesitate to do the work that is required of you. It's no coincidence that you are reading this book, if you take what you learn from here and apply it to your daily living and you keep obeying Father God, your spiritual maturity will increase. The blessings of spiritual growth is not only do people notice it, but the God the Father sees it and rewards it.

When the Holy Spirit convicts you of idols or idol worship, be sure not to ignore his conviction. That is the time to run to Father God and ask for help to let go of all idols and forms of idol worship. The Holy Spirit is a comforter, "convicter" and teacher. The Holy Spirit rests in each born again believer and is there to help guide us on the paths of righteousness. The Holy Spirit knows that we are up against a lot in these last and evil days, so it is important to be in tune with him. When the Holy Spirit warns us about someone or something, don't ignore it. He can warn us through speaking directly to us, through sudden fear coming on us (that does not easily go away), through signs that trouble is coming, he allows us to see people or things for who they really are! Maya Angelou said it best, "When someone shows you who they are, believe them the first time."

By knowing what the scriptures says about idols and idol worship, that is one of the best ways to help us avoid idolatry. God would not have us to be ignorant of the enemies devices. We know that:

1. **God's wrath was provoked,**
2. **Judgment pronounced, and**
3. **Punishment came when they sinned and worship idols made by their hands and foreign gods that could not save them!**

That's A SERIOUS WAKE UP CALL TO THE REST OF US! Times and cultures have changed, but GOD ALMIGHTY

REMAINS THE SAME. Since we know that idolatry is a serious offense before God, because it's the 1st and Greatest Commandment, let's not make excuses for the idols and idol worship in our lives, but remember the title of the book, It's Praying Time! & No More Idols!

Heavenly Father, thank you for giving me loving reminders to avoid the traps of idols and idol worship. I understand that cultures and society has changed, however Father God you are still the same. Father God would you help me to learn to worship you in my everyday lifestyle, choices, purchases and deeds? Almighty God, would you help me to study and memorize the scriptures against idols and idol worship? Please help me Lord God to stand flat footed on your Holy Word so I can avoid the temptation and traps of idols and idol worship. ABBA Father I desire to avoid idols and idol worship, please strengthen me in my mind, will and emotions to always desire to put you first. Father God would you please help me to obey you, and especially your First and Greatest Commandment in my public and private life? Would you bless me with an increase in discernment to always know how to avoid idols and idolatry in my life? In Jesus Mighty Name Amen and Amen.

Chapter 4 Summary

How Do We Avoid Idolatry?

- **Remember to live, pray and obey the 1st and Greatest Commandment.**

    - Matthew 22:36-38 NLT *"Teacher, which is the most important commandment in the law of Moses?" Jesus replied, "'You must love the LORD your God with all your heart, all your soul, and all your mind.' This is the first and greatest commandment.)* **then we will embrace it and allow the power of God to shape and mold us like never before.**

- **Desire to please God and ask him to help you live Matthew 22:36-38 in every area of your life. God will be first in our lives.**

- **Psalm 37:4 is a reminder to be captivated with joyfulness and thankfulness about the LORD, that he rewards us with the desires of our hearts.**

- **Worship through our everyday lifestyle of obedience to God's Holy Words and his commands.**

- Worship Father God with a pure and sincere heart, from wherever you are not just a certain time or place.

- Our worship with God the Father is consistent in both our public and private lives.

- When the Holy Spirit convicts us, let's run straight to God immediately and ask for the help that we need to let go and remove all idols and idol worship from our lives.

- Know what the scriptures says about the obedience and definitely the disobedience of idolatry.

Chapter 5
When Does Idolatry Occur?

When does idolatry (idol worship) occur? It occurs whenever we decide that someone or something else will occupy the majority of our time, energy and effort. Whenever we decide that God is not who we know him to be. Whenever we decide that God will not be first place in our lives whether through direct or indirect decisions, actions and conversations. Let's ask some questions to get one thinking about when idolatry occurs.

Who or what occupies the majority of your thoughts?

When there are set times at church for services, prayer, etc. are you available to be there?

Do you remember to spend time in prayer, reading the Bible, praise and worship on a daily basis?

Do you have an unhealthy obsession for sports, celebrities, TV shows, movies, gambling, food, eating?

Do you have any addictions that you have not been able to be set free of yet?

Another way of looking at is this. Does one ever say:

God understands that I have to work, and it's just too hard to turn down the overtime they are offering every weekend.

It does not take all of that, they are praying way too long.

How many songs does the choir or praise team have to sing?

God understands that we are late to church service the majority of the time.

Saturday or Sunday are the only days that I get to myself, I'm sleeping in, I'm taking that day or those days for myself to do whatever I want.

If I don't miss this church service, I won't have any "Me Time" to wash the car, get my hair done, etc.

It's okay, God understands that certain games come on during the church service and those are the services I will miss, because I have to watch the game live.

A certain celebrity is coming to town, so you don't pay your tithes and offerings so you can go to the concert.

You decide that when certain tickets go on sale for concerts, sporting events, etc. that you will camp out overnight so you can get the tickets.

You want to see the movie as soon as it comes out and so you decide that you won't go to church so you can see it.

Let's look at it another way. Are you on time (even early) for your job, concerts, movies, parties, clubs, bars, plays, and other events? Yet, when it is time to go to church services and rehearsals there is always a reason or excuse not to be on time. These questions were asked to help one see that a shift in priorities has to occur. Why is it okay to be late for what pertains to God and the things of God, yet be on time for just about everything else? God understands that we may encounter any number of things before leaving and while on the way to church, yet there shouldn't be an excuse every week though.

How can the choir sing too many songs or someone pray too long, if you have time to watch entire sporting events? Just to help see the timing involved on Bing.com it says that the average:

Baseball game is about **three hours**

Basketball game is between **two to three hours**

Football game about **three hours and fifteen minutes**

Concert is about **one and half to two hours**

Theatrical plays and **musicals** are about **two and half hours long**

Movies are about **one and half to three hours long**

People **camped outside for Black Friday sales, sporting events tickets, concert tickets**, etc. on average between **12 to 30 hours**

An **hair appointment** is about **one and half to three hours long**

Now that those times are laid out before us, we can see that outside of our everyday job or business that there are other things that consume quite a bit of our time. And let's be real when we are running too late for certain appointments we will be rescheduled for another day and time or forced to wait for a long time before they can get us in. The average **church service** is about **one or one and half hours long** and **Bible class** is usually about **45 minutes to one hour long**. It really is hard to say that you put God first when the hours don't add up or show/reflect that.

Sometimes it is a mindset that has to be overcome. Remember the world's culture overall is in direct opposition to the Word of God and Christian Faith. The way the world does things, more times than not is not the way a true believer does things. We are in this world but not of this world. God's mandated example and standards should be carried out on a daily basis.

The Global Pandemic was hard to watch and experience, but for those who know how fast life was going, it was good to slow down and really think about our lives. How we could do things better, what needed to change, what did we need to let go of, what did we need to start doing differently? That Global Pandemic was an eye opening experience on various levels, it gave many a lot more time to seek God in prayer and in Bible reading. Since we had to spend way more time at home, our excuses and even some responsibilities were taken from us and without any fault or control of our own.

Remember that God is a jealous God. **Who or what will stand in the place of the true and living God?** I am prayerful that we all know the answer is that no one or anything will stand in GOD'S RIGHTFUL PLACE. Our true worship belongs to only him and no one can take that from him. We have to stand for God even when it is not popular or the going trend of the masses. My prayer is also that the words in this book serve as a loving reminder, that if Father God is not first place in your life, that you will begin to pray and make the necessary adjustments to keep him first in every area of your life. In Chapter 6 there is an exercise that will help you to see where any other obvious or hidden idols might be in your life.

Whenever your heart is entangled to the point that you can't put God first that is an idol or idolatry. Whenever you give your all to everything and everyone but God that is idolatry.

Heavenly Father please help me to fully understand that no one or anything will stand in your place. Please give me a mind, heart and soul that won't allow me to be entangled with idols or idolatry (idol worship). Would you strengthen me to show you ABBA Father and this world that I give my all to you and you only? In Jesus Mighty Name Amen and Amen.

Chapter 5 Summary

When Does Idolatry Occur?

- **Whenever you decide in your heart, decisions and actions to put others and things before God.**

- **Whenever your heart is too entangled with others and things, that's idolatry.**

- **Whenever you worship people, places, things and money that is idolatry.**

- **Whenever you refuse to give God the time, money, energy and effort that he truly deserves. Remember God will not come 2nd Place, and definitely not last.**

Chapter 6
Where Does Idolatry Happen?

So, where does idolatry or idol worship occur? That's a really good question. So, let's look at it this way, where do you spend your time and where do you spend your money? In other words look at your calendar, organizer, day/night planner and write down how much time you spend on each activity. Have you ever tracked your time for a day or even a week to see what you spend your time doing? If you haven't how can you be for certain where the majority of your time is actually spent? The same goes for your money, do you track where you spend most of your money? Have you looked at your bank statement, credit card statement, receipts, tax returns, etc. to see where most of your money is spent? If you haven't done that how can you be for certain that you don't have "hidden idols" there?

The Christian faith walk should always be challenging us to be a better version of ourselves, but more precisely we should be striving to be more like Jesus Christ each day. There is work that is involved in our process to become more like Jesus Christ. We can dismiss it and say it does not take all of that, but the reality is it does take all of that and then some. Let this be a motivating challenge to you, start tracking your time and money from this day forward. Remember we are called to be Godly stewards over whatever God entrusts us with. One day we will have to give an account of how we managed what God gave to us.

What kinds of conversations do you spend your time on? What occupies your thoughts most of the time? Who do you talk about the most whether good or bad? Who do you follow the majority of the time? If we don't ask ourselves these questions on a daily or at a minimum a weekly basis it is very easy to get sidetracked and not even be aware that we are. What do I listen to the majority of the time? We have to remember that there are entry points to us:

1. **Eye gate (Who or what are you looking at?)**
2. **Ear gate (Who or what are you listening too?)**
3. **Mouth gate (Who or what are you talking about?)**
4. **Mind gate (Who or what are you thinking about?)**

The enemy knows that if he can get a hold of any one of these gates that it is easy to fall into the trap of idolatry or idol worship and not even be aware of it. **Remember what we put into this Christian journey, faith walk and relationship with Jesus Christ is what we will get out of it.** This is a loving reminder that we do not want to continue to live beneath the full privileges and promises of God. Sometimes we just need that encouraging reminder that we can do all things through Christ Jesus who strengthens us (Philippians 4:13)! So, even if this seems like a difficult task at first be reassured that you can track your time and money and tackle those "hidden and obvious idols" head on!

Before you continue reading this book please make the effort to track where you spend your time and money for at least seven days so you can have a better picture of how you spend your time and money for one whole week. Remember put the effort in and you will be glad that you did. My prayer is that you won't skip this activity as it will make it easier for you to answer the remaining questions in this chapter. Let's be committed to this process no matter what it shows you for the time being, because through prayer and determination you can conquer every idol in your life. **See pages 83 - 89**

Father God please give me the strength to track my time and finances for at least seven days and help me to stretch to a month if need be. Lord please give me supernatural focus, motivation and determination to complete this time and money tracker challenge. When I am tempted to give up please give me a SUPERNATURAL PUSH to keep going and complete the challenge with a spirit of excellence. Father God would you please forgive me for the idols and idolatry that I allowed to come into my life? Even when it is surprising what the challenge reveals please help me to remove

the obvious and hidden idols in my life. Holy Spirit thank you for convicting me and encouraging me to pray, obey and live the first and greatest commandments on a daily basis in Jesus Mighty Name Amen and Amen.

Ok now that you have tracked your time and money for one week, were you surprised at what you found? Or were you not surprised at all? Did you find this exercise to be of some value to you? If so, encourage others to do this challenge as well. If you did not, then I encourage you to think of ways to track your time and money that will help you to be aware when there is an idol problem.

Overall most of our largest purchases or payments are: mortgage, rent, car note, student loans, credit cards, tuition, medical bills, etc. God knows we need a place to stay, car to drive, education, healthcare, etc.; however we have a choice on those items. We need a nice and safe home; however we don't need a mansion unless we can afford it and have enough people to live there too. The same goes for the car we need a reliable and safe car to drive, but we don't need a very expensive one, especially if we really can't afford it either. What was the motive for that particular house or car purchase? If the motive was to get a lot of praise and applause from people, to try and impress people or to brag about what you have, then this is definitely idol territory.

Credit cards should be for an emergency, the enemy has trapped countless people with credit card debt. There is something manipulative about rewards programs that encourage you to spend more so you can get more rewards. Just imagine if you had no credit card debt at all, what you could do and accomplish with your money. Did you look at what you were charging on your credit cards? Were the purchases for necessities (things that you, your family or someone else needed and would be hard to live without)? Or were the purchases for wants (things that you, your family or someone else desires, things that you could live without)?

If there are more purchases for wants, again the motives for doing so comes into play as well. We have to remember that materialism is a sin. We live in a society that encourages us to spend and keep on spending and buying everything in sight. We have to be careful that we are in this world but not of it, there's nothing wrong with prospering but there is something wrong with not using our finances to advance the Kingdom of God.

My prayer is that as you tracked your finances that you saw your tithes and offerings being consistently paid to a church ministry or ministries. If you did not see that, please take a step of faith and commit to paying your tithes and offerings on a regular basis. My hope is that you commit to help people who are homeless, sick, persecuted and that quite possibly you invest in another trusted ministry as well. Learning to obey in every aspect is very important, especially since time is winding down we need to make the most of our financial investment in the Kingdom of God while we still have time to do so.

Ok so let's take another step and look at which purchases and payments are more than your tithes and offerings; and more than any other ministries or causes that you support. What would it take to change that if possible. Take for instance that you have a $400 cell phone bill for the family, there are ways to lower that bill and it might mean that you have to switch cell phone carriers to accomplish that. It might mean looking into what discounts do you qualify for through your job, car insurance, health insurance, AARP programs, SNAP, Medicaid, etc. With the money you save how could you use that to do more in advancing the Kingdom of God here on earth? Do you know someone who would like to go to Bible College but can't afford it? Do you know someone who could really use the financial assistance that you could provide? Is there another ministry that is doing a great work but needs financial support to continue?

As believers we say we love God, Jesus Christ and the Holy Spirit, but do the purchases and spending habits truly reflect that? Love is more than verbal; love is an action. Let's look at it another way. It would be hard for the mom, daughter and son to understand how the dad is spending more money and time on basketball, football, baseball and other interests than on them and with them. See it's hard to say that you really love your family but you don't ever do anything worthwhile for them or with them. Eventually the family figures out that you have a selfish kind of love for them. It won't be long before problems, conflicts and fights break out in that home. Why do we think we can treat Father God any differently? We know who and what we love, by where we spend our time and money.

I have heard countless testimonies of families who were upset that both parents or one of the parents spent so much time working to provide, that they forget to take time out with the family. The parents confused over providing and materialism for love, the children no matter how young or old want quality time with their parents. The parents say I bought them whatever they wanted. The children say you were never home, and you never made any of my games, never chaperoned a field trip, you were not there. We as believers have the power to change this before it's too late.

My prayer is that you spend more time praying, reading the Bible, praising and worshipping God and helping others while volunteering for a good cause. If you see that's not the case that you spend more time watching sports, television shows, movies, clubbing, bar hoping, cooking, eating, dancing, exercising, shopping, reading various books, talking on the phone, being on social media, gossiping, backbiting, bullying, etc. then you know it is time for a change in the right direction. Again I ask you, **"Who or what can stand in the place of the true and living God?"** If you are not loving God through your time and money, then you have to ask yourself why are these idols in the way?

I hope this challenge will motivate you to knock down every hidden and obvious idols that you may have in your life. God the Father wants a true intimacy with you, and that can't be achieved with idol worship in your life, no matter what form it comes in. Remember God is a jealous God, he will not come last in your life, so decide from this moment forward that you will put God first in every area of your life, even when it is hard you will no longer break the First Commandment of the Ten Commandments and the greatest commandment of all.

So in the exercise below please highlight in yellow where you spent time with God, where you spent time on Godly activities: soul winning, outreach – helping the poor, feeding the hungry, visiting the sick and shut in, visiting those in jail/prison, etc., clothing the poor, taking care of your family, etc. **(Hint the more yellow highlighting, the better; the less highlighting then it's time to pray and remove idols!)** Feel free to use extra piece of paper or a notebook to complete the challenge as well.

		Sunday	How much time?
		What did you do during this time?	
5am			
6am			
7am			
8am			
9am			
10am			
11am			
12pm			
1pm			
2pm			
3pm			
4pm			
5pm			
6pm			
7pm			
8pm			
9pm			
10pm			
11pm			
12am			
1am			
2am			
3am			
4am			

	Monday	
	What did you do during this time?	How much time?
5am		
6am		
7am		
8am		
9am		
10am		
11am		
12pm		
1pm		
2pm		
3pm		
4pm		
5pm		
6pm		
7pm		
8pm		
9pm		
10pm		
11pm		
12am		
1am		
2am		
3am		
4am		

	Tuesday	
	What did you do during this time?	How much time?
5am		
6am		
7am		
8am		
9am		
10am		
11am		
12pm		
1pm		
2pm		
3pm		
4pm		
5pm		
6pm		
7pm		
8pm		
9pm		
10pm		
11pm		
12am		
1am		
2am		
3am		
4am		

	Wednesday	
	What did you do during this time?	How much time?
5am		
6am		
7am		
8am		
9am		
10am		
11am		
12pm		
1pm		
2pm		
3pm		
4pm		
5pm		
6pm		
7pm		
8pm		
9pm		
10pm		
11pm		
12am		
1am		
2am		
3am		
4am		

	Thursday	
	What did you do during this time?	How much time?
5am		
6am		
7am		
8am		
9am		
10am		
11am		
12pm		
1pm		
2pm		
3pm		
4pm		
5pm		
6pm		
7pm		
8pm		
9pm		
10pm		
11pm		
12am		
1am		
2am		
3am		
4am		

	Friday	
	What did you do during this time?	How much time?
5am		
6am		
7am		
8am		
9am		
10am		
11am		
12pm		
1pm		
2pm		
3pm		
4pm		
5pm		
6pm		
7pm		
8pm		
9pm		
10pm		
11pm		
12am		
1am		
2am		
3am		
4am		

	Saturday	
	What did you do during this time?	How much time?
5am		
6am		
7am		
8am		
9am		
10am		
11am		
12pm		
1pm		
2pm		
3pm		
4pm		
5pm		
6pm		
7pm		
8pm		
9pm		
10pm		
11pm		
12am		
1am		
2am		
3am		
4am		

It's important to track our time because sometimes we can't see where it really goes, and WE CAN'T GET THAT TIME BACK, so being aware of how we spend our time, helps us not to waste as much time, and avoid idolatry!

The exercise for tracking our finances for every purchase do your best to get the receipt and place it in shoe box, folder, etc. for one whole week, then stretch to do a whole month. Add up the totals in tithes/offerings, charities, entertainment, clothing, etc. Another way you can do this exercise is tracking your bank statement(s) and credit card statement(s) to see where you are spending your money. What surprised you? How will you spend your money differently? Where could you save more money? How could you invest in the Kingdom of God?

Chapter 6 Summary

Where Does Idolatry Happen?

- Wherever we focus our time, money, energy and efforts more than we do on God and the things of God.

- Wherever we choose not to obey God and his commandments to have no other gods, or love Father God with our whole heart, mind and soul.

- We can't say we love God without obeying him.

    - 1 John 5:3 TPT, True love for God means obeying his commands, and his commands don't weigh us down as heavy burdens.

    - 1 John 5:3 AMP For the [true] love of God is this: that we habitually keep His commandments and remain focused on His precepts. And His commandments and His precepts are not difficult [to obey].

- Protect the gates to our mind, heart and soul.

    - Eye Gate, Ear Gate, Mouth Gate & Mind Gate

- From time to time, track your time and money to see do you have obvious and hidden idols that need to be removed immediately.

- Who or what will stand in the place of the true and living God?

Chapter 7

Summary & Salvation Prayer

Thank you for going on this journey to a better understanding that there can be NO MORE IDOLS. When we see things the way God sees them, then we are headed in the right direction. Idolatry is a serious offense before God and provokes the wrath of God. God asks us in the scripture and even today, "Why would you praise and worship idols that cannot heal or save you in the day of trouble?"

Who or what will stand in the place of the true and living God in our lives? The answer is no one. God deserves first place in our lives and once we have a better understanding of his Holy Words that should make it easier to release every idol and all forms of idol worship from our lives. The scriptures lets us know we can't say we truly love God, and not obey him. Anyone who has had the honor of being a child remembers that your parents required that you obeyed them. When you did not obey there were consequences, like punishments (being grounded, spankings, no television for weeks, etc.) and when you did obey there were rewards (dessert treats, movie nights, money, gifts, etc.).

God really has simplified this life journey that we are on, but we have to obey God and his Holy Word.

God knows that if your love, attention and adoration is focused too much on any one person and/or things it will lead you astray from him. Father God knows best and has given us a roadmap to navigate this world that we live in. We now know when we worship, love and obey God that even when we suffer it will work for our good, but overall God will bless us and even send prosperity but we have to stick to His Holy Word. The opposite is true, when idols or idolatry are in our lives, serious punishment is coming if we don't take heed to God's warnings. **Psalm 115:1 GNT To you alone, O Lord, to you alone, and not to us, must glory be given because of your constant love and faithfulness.**

On the next few pages are some idolatry scriptures that will be useful to pray, meditate, memorize and live as one walks on this journey.

Idolatry Scriptures

Leviticus 19:4 AMP *Do not turn to idols or make for yourselves molten gods (images cast in metal); I am the LORD your God.*
Leviticus 26:1 GNT *The LORD said, "Do not make idols or set up statues, stone pillars, or carved stones to worship. I am the LORD your God.*

2 Chronicles 24:18-19 AMP *They abandoned the house of the LORD, the God of their fathers, and served the Asherim and the idols; so [God's] wrath came on Judah and Jerusalem for their sin and guilt. Yet God sent prophets among them to bring them back to the LORD; these prophets testified against them, but they would not listen.*

Psalm 97:7 GNT *Everyone who worships idols is put to shame; all the gods bow down before the LORD.*

Psalm 106:36 GNT *God's people worshiped idols, and this caused their destruction.*

Psalm 115:4-8 GNT *Their gods are made of silver and gold, formed by human hands. They have mouths, but cannot speak, and eyes, but cannot see. They have ears, but cannot hear, and noses, but cannot smell. They have hands, but cannot feel, and feet, but cannot walk; they cannot make a sound. May all who made them and who trust in them become like the idols they have made.*

Psalm 135:15-18 KJV The idols of the heathen are silver and gold, the work of men's hands. They have mouths, but they speak not; eyes have they, but they see not; They have ears, but they hear not; neither is there any breath in their mouths. They that make them are like unto them: so is every one that trusteth in them.

Ezekiel 14:3-8 GNT *"Mortal man," he said, "these men have given their hearts to idols and are letting idols lead them into sin. Do they think I will give them an answer?" "Now speak to them and tell them what I, the Sovereign LORD, am saying to them: Each of you Israelites who have given your heart to idols and let them lead you into sin and who then come to consult a prophet, will get an answer from me—the answer that your many idols deserve! All those idols have turned the Israelites away from me, but by my answer I hope to win back their loyalty. "Now then, tell the Israelites what I, the Sovereign LORD, am saying: Turn back and leave your disgusting idols. "Whenever one of you Israelites or one of you foreigners who live in the Israelite community turn away from me and worship idols, and then go to consult a prophet, I, the LORD, will give you your answer! I will oppose you. I will make an example of you. I will remove you from the community of my people, so that all of you will know that I am the LORD.*

2 Corinthians 16:16-18 GNT *How can God's temple come to terms with pagan idols? For we are the temple of the*

living God! As God himself has said, "I will make my home with my people and live among them; I will be their God, and they shall be my people."
And so the Lord says, "You must leave them and separate yourselves from them. Have nothing to do with what is unclean, and I will accept you. I will be your father, and you shall be my sons and daughters, says the Lord Almighty."

Revelation 9:20 GNT *The rest of the human race, all those who had not been killed by these plagues, did not turn away from what they themselves had made. They did not stop worshiping demons, nor the idols of gold, silver, bronze, stone, and wood, which cannot see, hear, or walk.*

1 John 5:21 KJV *Little children, keep yourselves from idols. Amen.*

1 John 5:21 NLT *Dear children, keep away from anything that might take God's place in your hearts.*

1 John 5:21 AMP *Little children (believers, dear ones), guard yourselves from idols—[false teachings, moral compromises, and anything that would take God's place in your heart].*

1 John 5:21 AMPC Little children, keep yourselves from idols (false gods)—[from anything and everything that would occupy the place in your heart due to God, from

any sort of substitute for Him that would take first place in your life].

1 Timothy 6:10 KJV For the love of money is the root of all evil: which while some coveted after, they have erred from the faith, and pierced themselves through with many sorrows.

Heavenly Father, as I seek to grow in a better intimacy with you, I ask for the strength to continue to renounce and denounce all idols and idolatry in my life. As I obey you, please help me to share my praise report and testimony so others can overcome their idols and idolatry too. Lord God I desire to be utilized for your glory to help set others free from idol worship and paganism. Help me to remember as I live an idol free life before men, women, and children I help to bring you the glory in the first and greatest commandment, to have no other gods before you, and to love you with my whole heart, mind, and soul. I declare my obedience will be known and seen by the world, that I kept the faith in the true and living God. I am determined to glorify and magnify you, Father God especially each day of my life from this moment forward in Jesus Mighty Name Amen and Amen.

We want to make the most of every opportunity to win souls for Jesus Christ. The truth is eternity is closer for some than others. We are not just living for this life, but we are surely living for the life to come. Let me encourage you do not delay in saying this Salvation Prayer. Please repeat this prayer from a sincere heart.

Dear Lord Jesus, I know that I am a sinner, and I ask you for your forgiveness. I believe you died for my sins and rose from the dead. I turn from my sins, and invite You to come into my heart and life. I ask for the Holy Spirit to dwell in me, to guide me, and to teach me all things. I choose to trust and follow You as the Son of God and LORD and Savior in Jesus name Amen and Amen.

If you repeated that prayer with a true sincerity you JUST GOT SAVED!!! We encourage you to read your Bible on a daily basis. Here are your next steps:

1) **Download the free Bible App** <https://www.youversion.com/the-bible-app/>.
2) **Get a paper Parallel Study Bible that has King James Version(KJV) and another version of your choice that helps you to understand the scriptures better.**
3) **Read the Bible every day.**
4) **Ask God the Father to lead you to a church home where the Bible is taught and preached in a way that you can understand it and live it out daily.**

Lastly if you repeated the Salvation Prayer and got saved please email us at itsprayingtime2020@gmail.com, we would like to pray for you and encourage you along your spiritual journey. You can also email us your prayer requests and we would be glad to stand in the gap for you.

Author's Biography

Dr. Kimberly K. Clayton is determined to keep God in first place in her life. She is currently working on another biblical project with goals to represent Jesus Christ to the fullest, win as many souls for Jesus Christ as possible, recruit and train additional godly intercessors, and to continue to pray and intercede as God has called her to do. She lives with her daughter, Elise, who is her pride and joy!

She is the founder and leader of "It's Praying Time," a ministry where prayer intercession and training takes place on a weekly basis. Dr. Kimberly believes in the power of prayer and intercession and is determined to help others grow in this calling through the prayer line, Facebook Live and YouTube. You are welcome to become a subscriber to our "It's Praying Time" You Tube Channel. "It's Praying Time" is focused on reaching as many people as possible for Jesus Christ through various means and platforms.

Dr. Kimberly Clayton is also an ordained and licensed minister through the "School of the Prophet" which is led by their fearless leader, Prophetess Renee Gordon. One of Kimberly's most prized moments is when she and her young daughter, Elise, had their second baptism together through the "School of the Prophet". She also treasures being able to serve on other prayer lines when needed.

www.ingramcontent.com/pod-product-compliance
Lightning Source LLC
Chambersburg PA
CBHW051947160426
43198CB00013B/2339